MY HUMAN COMEDY

MY HUMAN COMEDY

THE MAN FROM SASKATCHEWAN BOOK TWO

Gerald Hill

COTEAU BOOKS

Edited by Jeanette Lynes.
Book and cover design by Duncan Campbell.
Cover image: *Face and Bird* by Wieslaw Rosocha/Veer.

Printed and bound in Canada at Gauvin Press.
This book is printed on 100% recycled paper.

Recycled
Supporting responsible use of forest resources
www.fsc.org Cert no. SGS-COC-2624
© 1996 Forest Stewardship Council

LIBRARY AND ARCHIVES CANADA CATALOGUING IN PUBLICATION

Hill, Gerald, 1951-
My human comedy : the man from Saskatchewan, book two / Gerald Hill.

Poems.
ISBN 978-1-55050-371-5

I. Title. II. Title: Man from Saskatchewan, book two.

PS8565.I443M9 2008 C811'.54 C2008-901474-X

10 9 8 7 6 5 4 3 2 1

COTEAU BOOKS

2517 Victoria Ave.
Regina, Saskatchewan
Canada S4P 0T2

AVAILABLE IN CANADA & THE US FROM
Fitzhenry & Whiteside
195 Allstate Parkway
Markham, ON, Canada, L3R 4T8

The publisher gratefully acknowledges the financial assistance of the Saskatchewan Arts Board, the Canada Council for the Arts, the Government of Canada through the Book Publishing Industry Development Program (BPIDP), Association for the Export of Canadian Books, and the City of Regina Arts Commission, for its publishing program.

Canada Council for the Arts Conseil des Arts du Canada
Saskatchewan Arts Board
Canada
Regina City of Regina

Contents

IV

V

VI

for the lover

I

Whose love is great as the sky is blue,
the sky is blue,
the sky is.

Invocation

I call all sparrows to pull
shadows from the parking lot
so the light gets to me (balconied,
needy for your warmth).

I call on the Sysco truck with case-lots
of condiments for the restaurant to rev
at maximum rpms and thus drown
my whining.

I call all passers-by who take
the garbage out, bring home coffee
or booze, or wait at the bus stop
to fan out and find you, carry you here.

I call bored high school kids at noon
to eat their fast food swiftly
so I may taste your slow
circling tongue.

A sub store worker wrestles with a friend.
A dumpster spills.
Light sends boisterous
signals for you, that is what's
doing it, the light is.

And now that you're gone
I call all rain clouds to publicize
these moments after rain.

Song for the Same Old Sky

Under the front seat of your Oldsmobile
there it was, a broken piece you forgot.

Late afternoon afraid to find
more light you close the blinds until
sky's the size of a single
bright word.

You drink tea on your balcony
to the woman you love to kiss, the sky
on your shoulder is that warm.

When you go to remember
the sky's an empty attitude *whatever,*
you can have it all.

Just north of where the sun
will set, the bright fringe of dark clouds
tosses, beyond that the shape
of top hats nods to clear space, in the south
a backbone of clouds.

Morning takes all night to come home.

Whatever else you think
you want to say,
the sky's all that.

Road to Raymore: A Poetic

A coda in a clarinet concerto rips.
A fenceline shakes until its strands snap free, suave
but manic enough, barbed arms etching
grooves in the morning air. No line should imply
so certainly the next, as if the earth had four
corners or a woman small children whose hair
must be combed the same way.

Some clarinets stay low,
gut it out down there, refuse
to give into melody. These are
my heroes, stepping on tones,
thinking on one plane, playing
another, tunes like rusty water
lingering a drain.

Give me that broken clarinet, that mind.

Road to Raymore: The Beliveau Hour on CBC Radio

After an hour of music selected by Jean Beliveau, the great Montreal Canadiens captain

In the Beliveau Hour, the valley opens to pale
greens and yellows – cattle, a farmhouse,
pasture, the odd semi, oxbows like
a necklace on the rouged fields,
the edges of the pond so green
my thighs hurt.

In the Beliveau Hour, the last two curves
of an inlet lead to a pond, the creek so shiny
I warm myself in the look of it, and now
Scarlatti and Béla Fleck, banjo as
quirky mandolin.

The Beliveau Hour includes a graveyard
north of Southey, auto wreckers, shadows making
faces in the ponds and canola trying to
yellow up the sky.

By the end of the hour one ridge of trees
slides behind the other, stones show up
white and smooth in the pastures,
flax stalks electric in its field, all of this
easy as gravel to see.

Becoming and Going: An Oldsmobile Story

Up the north hill of the Qu'Appelle Valley,
breaking the spell of the trees even
the dead ones, thinking *plenty of water*
so far this year, hot though,
and everywhere evidence of wind,
I'm pointing skyward in my Oldsmobile
when I'll be damned there's Dad
in his '58 Chev pulling in behind me,
lifting one finger to wave.

He drives a little faster. Right away he passes,
one hand on the wheel, elbow out
the window, right arm back over
the top of the seat, hawks in the air
or in his mind and he's singing
a hymn to pass the miles, thinking
berries and milk, thinking Alice.

We get a good look at each other. I must seem
older, he's the same. We understand
as much as we ever did, two cars
reaching up the hill toward Southey,
learning each other's speed.

The sun dodges in and out of clouds, strictly
ornamental, a '50s sky. Ponds and sloughs
cruise, the highway swerves by farms, crops pale
as wind. *Everything is planted now*
we wait, he might think, remembering more
roads like this one, open, not much shoulder
but plenty of curves, the land
flexing its light. He carries what he needs
at cocktail hour: bottle of rye or Jamaican rum
in a case with a jigger and glasses. *Good to see you,*

Don, his friends must have said. *Good to see you*
again, Dad, I'm thinking, and now a third car
comes into my rear view – my son Tom
in his mother's Camry.

His wave is cool, casual. He settles on my tail,
ready to pass, blow by the Oldsmobile
for good (though he'll wait for the divided
highway) and I play along, throw back the glare I use
on senior drivers in the city. He's playing
Red Hot Chili Peppers, heading for
a date with that red-haired beauty of his
after work tonight or one of those
barbecues with J. and the boys, the deep-freeze
empty when they're done.

I wish my Dad could speak with him,
shoot some pool, decide who should quarterback
the Riders this year. Up ahead, Dad
sends advice for Tom through
his rear-view mirror to me –

– serve your guests their first drink,
after that they're on their own
– sit up straight
– if you're hungry, eat a piece of bread and butter
– hitchhikers aren't free, they're tied to the road –

old-fashioned, the advice always seemed
even to me. But Dad, I respect where
it comes from. I wish you could know Tom
loves the highway, and knows
how to take a good bow. His many friends
love him, and like all Hill men, at least the two
before him, wouldn't he rather
be playing ball?

By the time I get to Watson, I see
darker clouds north and east
sunlight in patches and no more
cars on the road.

Stan Still's Notes Toward an Empty Space

He has been there but isn't now.
It remembers him, a field of blue air
weeping with room.
                    For two dollars he'll hit
golfballs through it.
                    If he doesn't know what
to say he'll make something up.
                              Tools, extra lumber,
scrap, used cars, fluid, weeds and tall grass, gravel, concrete
foundations.
               The space carries fragments
of a mind's real eyes, a field on which one
team enters as the other leaves.
                              Former players feel
the game the way they used to and think
they'll still succeed.
                    From the highway
the field appears green but less so, briefer leaves
warm for the last time, this field crossed
by someone he's never known, not that
he's ever known.

Mornings

I *road next to a field*

Most of the day is open sky and a man who takes
his shirt off, half buries himself in sunlight, a swelter
of new cones high in the spruce. The sweetness pours
off him. Let's see, will it be a wrecked machine he climbs, pretends to start,
drives? And the breeze pours off him. He's got a nose for crows,
a blackness in him.

He's seen fifty summers but just one
sun, this one, the wild blue goner, and he burns
if he sits long enough, a man bitten,
blood pouring off him.

It's hard to make a difference in this heat
shoving against itself. The man deserves
where he comes from, that highway
town where the sun is.

2 *pond*

He waits in shade by the water,
ready like scent for holy flowers. This wait drives him crazy.
One, it spreads. Two, he's stuck with slits of light on the water,
stillness and all. Three, what's it for? He hears
his brothers-in-law say *Get to work, you dog.*

He gets quieter every morning, like an old man pulled under a day
at a time into murk, debris, damselflies tethered
like the Hindenburg, the usual systems of brightness and stone,
and a liquid edge beginning to end it all. He hears his father
say *It's just a matter of time.*

And the only way out is to settle in like birds
he doesn't know, the *padillio-padillio* bird, the *rico-rico-*
rico bird, the bird heard in his next lover's yard. *If*
you're lucky he hears her say.

The future stirs when a wind picks up, same wind as
yesterday.

3 *garden*

He sleeps when he dreams, wakes up, goes out. An early
hour's shadow shrinks east across a field, a few sheets
short of a cloudless sky. It's do or die, the day
grows a view of a garden with a sparrow
across it, flutter in the corn rows, heart-shaped
potatoes, shy flowers. He gives up and starts
today tomorrow.

Again the day gets to him in a hurry.
He sits tight against the weather, his notebook lashed
to his knee, snags his sleeve on the east wind,
could taste, if he wanted to, rain. Wind
walks into his eyes, the sky
a utility grade.

So the night pulls off him. He hears himself think, thinks it's crows
or a wind venting. The field scribbles light, shadow.
The sun rises from the names of sleepless
birds, *baw-doo, baw-doo.*

He's got the dream at his back. He said
something funny and he's laughing now, the train
in the distance a soft chord. Nothing's original,
dreams had it first, the garden
has grown. By morning the dream
expels the dreamer.

4 *junkyard*

On a bench made from bed frames he considers
the principles of fiction – manufacture,
use, abandonment. That's how stories get to junk's
weedy avenues.

He claims he'll end up here himself and that
his sorry misdeeds belong here. Way past ending,
he keeps getting started in this faraway
station, aluminum, barrels of brass. He's spare,
like parts. In this fatal rust, he writes down theories of decay
and fall, his findings.

Will he drive away in the '53 International?
Will he steal a toolbox?
Is he burning yet?

5 *cornfield*

Shot of thunder, shot of rain, clean wind,
any old sky will do. His son said he's rollerblading with Lisa today
and could he please have a poem written for him
and read over the phone to him, also today?
His son wants something with cars in it, a brand new
key to his mother's Camry. In a year or two he'll drive
to sunset on a gravel road.

A year or two after that out of respect for morning
he'll walk along the corn, feeling about knee-high
and at the bottom of every day come home.

6 *graveyard*

He was born when he fell in love and every
time he's alive again, six feet under the stars, his voice
in her hair, it's love looking through him.

He's full of stillness or is it love
that's simple, what you have to do to get here,
forty feet from the newest stones.

The love of the poet always comes to ill
fortune. A sucker for love, he'll die of it. *When he fell*
in love, his stone will say. *When he kissed*
her hair, how close the stars were, and
the rest.

II

I can't see anything else but you,
only you,
the sky is.

Falling

Love is like this morning
only sooner. Like a bird, I've found
the feeder, hopped
for bits of you.

Falling in love my body
loosens, my mind peels, dreams
multi-coloured wires from which sparrows
unsettle. Which way is supper? I eat
whatever inches to my plate, dress like smoke,
invent happiness, assume every one
of my plants will grow. Haven't been
in love like this since Judy
played piano in grade four.

The hotel curtains close. We're in rooms
109 to 300, trying
each other on. And love like light
turns clean as we'll ever be.

How Stan Still Got His Name

You don't want to look stupid?
You're half-way to looking stupid
every minute you don't change his name.
— BRENDA SCHMIDT

Something tapped at Stan like a drummer,
made him open the blind to look out.
The afternoon exploded. Stan
ducked but was out there and ready
when the next bright motor came along,
pulling him by the eyes. Stan had learned
surrender to such moments is good
in moderation, but too much surrender
next thing you know the giant hawks
are picking you off the field.

Stan could see the fencepost he was named after,
though there is some falseness to the story.
Stan's mother did not have to grip a post
in the throes of labour at Stan's birth
by the barley field. Nor did Stan's dad
see Stan pound in his first post
at the age of four and a half. The true
explanation of Stan's name is that
his uncle came to visit,
took one look at the newborn and said
He looks like that fencepost over there.

My Career

I am the greatest hockey player ever
to skate out of Herbert, Saskatchewan,
even stumble out, my blades rarely
parallel. You can't count
on the fingers of one sweaty hand
the trophies I should have won. My ears ache
and my body, which used to ache, now glides across
any line so smoothly you'd think
I'd written it.

                    Wearing my pads like a shield,
I'm named for a great king. Lesser players
better kneel. If not, I show them
the dipsy-doodle, give them a cuff
on the back of the head, flick a razor-sharp
backhand to a teammate streaking for the net.
Two or three times already this happened in my career.
Under the Herbert flag, a cloud-shaped
field of blue and green, I'm asked
on TV what I'm thinking. I can't believe
what's happening, and say so.
But I want to say Hi to Doris and Mom
and Dad, I love you guys, I'll be there soon.
Down King Street I'll parade to the station house
with my skates, my broken sticks,
a couple of pucks, and my all-star jersey – *Alfred,*
the back of it says.

Song for the Rock Dove

If I'd have known you were once
hunted for meat I wouldn't
sour at the splotches of white
shit the size of a baking cup
you left on my hockey gear or complain
on Sunday morning you're all I hear
ten feet above me on the roof.

Your "varied colouration" no doubt is nurtured
by how you spend your time, what you
pick up with your pigeony beak. I was hasty
blaming you for the ruin of my deck chair
which Lucy and I painted light blue and then
for forty days and forty nights
you shit on.

What do I know about migration
to North America four hundred
years ago, how distressing that might be
so yes, I'm inspired to climb
onto the roof with a basket
of whatever doves love.

Though you're worse than the goddam wind
I admit that in the heat of a June afternoon
on this balcony overlooking the Travelodge parking lot
when I take off my shirt (I've evolved
a century or two myself) I don't mind
the script you splatter on my indoor-
outdoor carpet or my barbecue. I give you
one of my five or six sweetest
Latin names.

To Day

Good day, day. What a find of crows you rip the air
with this morning. How did the night go, did wings
dream you double, fly you down the ribbing
of a long black tube? As for me, thanks for asking, I dreamed
old professor Paul gave me nothing higher
than 72. 72! What's that, cool night in Pensacola? So,
how are you, today. I see the garden is still
dill and the clouds breathe lightly, otherwise
yesterday all over, right? Oops, shouldn't have mentioned
yesterday. Ate some bad saskatoons. Hey what's with
the dew, dude? Just got out of bed, have to dry
my feet, start over. Feeling fine? Let's have
a look at your tongue, hmm.

I'm guessing sunlight later, shades and
bright ways. I'm guessing air so sweet, married
women will breathe it. (And between you and me I wouldn't mind
breathing one of them.) Looks like butterflies want to be
see-through flowers in the sun's high shine.
The cars that get here will go. And some of this
dust is going to move. A flag of a day. Well, got to run.
For sure, see you later.

My Cock

The Heavenly Messenger "makes a sign
that I should keep my silence
and bow down."
— DANTE, *The Divine Comedy*, TRANS. JOHN CIARDI

It's hard to speak the truth about my cock.
What if the truth isn't big enough?
What if the truth about my cock lets me down?
He's part wonder, part crow, part ah
what the hell, let's do it. First thing
every morning – stout as a rainbarrel or meek
as a folded canoe – he *is* first thing in the morning. I don't
invent him, rub-a-dub-dub, he's there.
Like the so-called gopher he's quick to rise,
ready for danger, gentle in both or
either of your hands.

He likes your attention. In fact,
he likes you to gather around. Go ahead, reach out
and touch your personal God of War. Call him Noah
Doubtaboutit, your only man. Call him
Planet Jr. or Westbound train. Like your own lips, he's yours.

My cock's travelled everywhere, a regular Jan Morris.
But he always comes home to the sound
he began with, c-c-cock. Are you nervous?
Don't be. My cock is innocent, like sunlight
sparking off fourteen feet of irrigation steel. Don't blame
the cock for the man that stands behind it.
He done you wrong, the cock just done you.

But the cock gets lonely, folded away half
the time (except twice a week
at the tanning salon when the cock
in its porcelain tube, The Grooveyard,
bakes to a deep bronze). We're talking
my cock, don't forget. I call it mine, but you
can call it yours. You could call it up, put my
hand there, yours, each other's hand. Oh yes.
My cock remembers nosing for sounds
your body makes. In dreams he's still at it, hearing you.

Just wind

If I chew grass, I chew wind. It follows.
Right between the eyes and just above there's a spot
wind is holy, any wind.

The world is full of nothings that I name
because I feel them – heat and armies of grass,
rhubarb in its sloping huts, dash of crow –
in the middle of the afternoon exposing
myself to wind writing *dry*
(taste of wind).

*

Some guys, they write a poem,
they have to sit where they sat
yesterday to change it.
If yesterday the wind blew
and today it doesn't they're screwed.
So they call it Part Two or even just
2 by itself, these poets. They'd rather not finish a poem
because then it wouldn't be as long.
Why the hell would you ever want
to finish? the poets say,
shifting in their chairs. *Love is why*
we speak at all, and no, it's never over because
here she comes again and the poets sit
back and the grass nods
dimly in yesterday's breeze.

*

Give poets an hour, they give it back
pinned to five-six pages they call the right touch
of clouds, wind, cabbage, whatever's there, butterfly
spasms, tensions of corn. *Not*
quite, say the poets. *It's all*
about love. Huh? *The lover,* they say,
we always speak to, like it or not. Well,
Ok, whatever, the poets are looking away again.

It must have something to do with time. I suppose
it follows. If the poets sit down
same time every afternoon, it *is*
the same time, and they can practice
its passing routines.

These poets fall asleep with their eyes open.
Grass becomes illusion, blur, which poets like,
thinking they've pierced the surface of things,
and they'd rather not end so they'll damn well
sit there till they don't.

*

All poets believe their eyes for a moment.
Then they might as well not see at all, they're busy
writing it down. Isn't that wild? They want the world
clear and out of the way. They think of themselves
as islands in a sea of wind and a line later
they're rhubarbarians with black books, heating
their feet in soil, rubbing at the air with their broad
wise hands. Those hallelujahs are the poets
feeling good about the wind feeling
light, grass directing this whole scene.

If you see poets
facing what they're doing, say *nothing,*
stop there.

*

A poplar died trying to grow
sideways in the shade of
a healthy tree. Poets love the touch
of mould, the helplessness, the kick-ass
thrill of looking it over, a mob
of poets looking so hard the shell
of the poplar gives up and topples.
And the poets ask,
Where else can we see what light
means but in these branches, ending
at phantom leaves?

It's always light, this time of day when the poets
sit in their plastic chairs, offering to make
something of the breeze, the non-breeze
vibrations in the grass, a vigil of longing
under the sign of the tree.

*

Wind's a bully and the poets,
like Virgil in Dante's hell, order it low
in its black boat to wait there till it's needed.
Poets are lucky to make words
do that sort of thing. The wind's
a scary place but it's just wind – remote,
hard up for stillness, pushing through light
like it's not there, rushing like a bell to half past.
Poets of the world, you might
think yourselves endangered,
the wind blowing hard against your shield,
blowing down the words hung on your walls.

*

The poets are old men with two canes
who suck on a stalk of rhubarb they can barely bend
low enough to break. They've learned what they can give
of themselves, what to withhold under the hats
they wear, rhubarb their mainline from sunlight to need.

The poets give themselves time in the garden,
long as they can move their rickety knees,
hoeing with their canes, wary of a gang of crows.
Hoeing, digging with their canes, the sun hot enough
they can say they worked in it. Then back
to their poor houses in a slow procedure,
one cane, the other cane, until a young
woman walks by, and the poets get frisky
in what passes for a hurry. They talk, have
a laugh, show her for a few sad arcs how
their canes work as sickles. *Pretty good,*
she says but she's got to go and the poets too,
out of the heat though they wouldn't mind
staying out longer.

*

The poets in their green plastic chairs line the north
edges of the garden the next afternoon, wave
to whoever passes to the south. What they think
will be what they see, as usual, the tension
of their inner lives outed. *We're trapping*
gophers with our eyes, do you mind?
There are no gophers today. Maybe
dust will do, that sky up there,
a line or two after that.

The poets want to see themselves
in the stunts one day pulls on the one before.
They whistle, speak aloud, raise a little
dust among the corn.

*

The garden's all right as it is, tended
and watered. Can the same be said
of the poets? One of them trembles,
one of them bites off grass, another
thinks he sees heat quiver in the corn.
These are accidental signs of life.

The poets seem to be wasting away on blue.
They want to make it page seven
in the books they write, near
the beginning, it would have to be, this blue.

They sit up in their chairs, ready
as they'll ever truly be.

III

Storm spills over the alley drains,
the sky is rain,
the sky is.

Rain

I know the rain was you
it blew so finely
I went to school to learn to read

an old school circa 1912
red brick from the seams of the prairie
draws rain

and just as it always was in school
I wake up to the darker shades of field
when a shower passes through

then on to the ending
rain breeze
we feel in the same sky

Distant Weather

Plans to build a house of nothing but sound fell through
after the first long pause of an entranceway,
dreamed crows mounted over the door.

Workers who had arrived by bus that morning
hovering in their accents
stopped making and let it go –

the highway hallway
the windows with death between their panes
foundation of hums

and every other silence a room
in which they faced distant weather
painting the walls with trains and hanging bells

otherwise doubting their own voices
abandoned
to the sound of hammers.

Alice Kicks Butt at Crystal Lake

In red and white T-shirts @ $4.98 apiece
Mom challenged the Jones family
to a game of ball for the all-you-can-eat
chicken buffet at the campground diner.

Tell you what, the biggest of the Jones boys said.
We're hungry. Let's make it a one-inning game.
Sounds good, Mom said, slicing a melon.
You can bat first.

Mom sent her brother Wallace out to field.
Take your bike, she said. *We need you to cover*
some ground out there, and young Alf,
whose ticker'd been acting up, took first base.

Pearl said she'd play both second and third,
and Edith, who played some ball before the war,
would pitch, though unsure she could chuck
that far. *I'll catch,* Mom hollered. *Play ball.*

A half-inning later it was 44-nothing and would have been worse
if Wallace hadn't ridden under three fly balls. *All right,*
get the bats going, Mom said, *and help yourself*
to that rhubarb crisp of June's.

For Mom with her walker, loose sand around second
was a problem, and Alf with his weak heart
had to walk from base to base but Wallace
was a terror on that PathGrinder mountain bike,

fish-tailing doubles into triples, scoring easily
on the overthrows – it was 44–20 just like that.
Even so, they were down to their last out when Alf
called time and took a case of Blue to the Jones boys.

That'll keep 'em nice and loose, Alf said,
and the rally resumed. Pearl bounced another base hit,
and Edith legged out a slow roller.
Mom slashed a double down

the rightfield line, 44–23. Mom and her brothers
and sisters all knew what home meant
and how to get there, 44–27.
Under a sky like this they were all at home –

the air sweet, the land looking full, 44–32. *Great
T-shirts, Alice,* Wallace said, when Edith slipped home
with their 38th run. In fact, they didn't like staying away
from home for long, and that's what won it for them,

touching home plate so quietly. *It's nothing,* they said
later at the diner, laughing at each other's stories,
filling in the names, all the way to angel food cake
with peaches and a single glass of white wine each.

That was quite the game, they all said, sharing a toast.
For a while there, I wasn't sure we'd catch them.

Before and After Trains, a Fifty-cent Piece

Before

As the sky is my witness, dusty and dazed,
the Queen lies face down, shiny
on the CN line. It's trespass, *uh-uh,*
uh-uh, go crows over the Queen's hot rails.

Alone for once, the Queen presses her cheek to the forty
feet of hard Algoma steel. She's queen without shadow,
more lowness than highness but radiant
in her radii, her coat of arms, two lions mounting a rosebush
at the base of a flagpole. Does she really long to reign
over us? Soon, thin as a whistle, she'll feel
a rumbled *hip-hip-hooray.* I know I'll throw
my hat in the air, the protocol when Her Majesty
melts under a westbound train.

After

Busted by a thousand tons out of Canora she's ex-
jewel in a creosote palace, a spike groupie in a rail bed,
the so-so sovereign formerly known
as Princess. Her eyes if they hadn't disappeared
would cloud like the dull side of a royal
seal the size of empty sockets. Ringed by crushed
Latin she's a blank micro-monarch, illegal
tender. She waves to only the sky and me, oh rue,
rue Britannia.

Anecdote of the New Bookshelf

Before the first book is placed, the shelves
breathe their empty minds in the silent room,
carpet new, before all alphabet, but here comes Abley,
Alford and half an armload of Atwoods. So the rose
of emptiness fades.

Waiting in loose piles on the floor below, Schmidt
leans on Schoemperlen, Wah
on Wallace while the Wiebes,
Armin and Rudy, and the Wilsons,
Ethel, Sheri-D and Paul, chat away as if
waiting for a ferry, unaware that a metre or so
above them, the lines have come unruled –

*Mc*s balk at standing with *M*s, McAdam
bickers with McCourt. Lunn and Lynes comment
smugly from the shelf above. Kroetsch,
further back, horses around as usual. McKay spreads
rumours about Margoshes and Marlatt.
The Mitchells, Ken and W.O., press ahead aggressively
until Pollock for all Ps says *far enough.* Soon the books,
one thicker or taller (maybe just louder) than the next,
elbow one another, flaunt their fonts, bring
the whole bookcase down.

No new carpet, no matter how deep,
can absorb such a blow.
The sub-floor caves in, apartment collapses, books
in their porous jackets wash away in a rare rain
to the newly deepened lake, where some of them settle,
spines up, in the goose shit and mud.
A few of the lighter ones drain
through the creek to the South Sask
river all the way to Hudson's Bay and oceans
beyond, where a few even now refuse
the shore.

                    Back in the rubble
of suite 25 the shelves lie empty again, born
like all of us to carry – sometimes fall from –
the weight of our own poor words.

Prayer for the Sun

Not that my teapot is full of rain or that
it runs from the corners of my mouth and a man
carrying trash to the burn barrel wears a peaked cap
and the spark in the cylinders of my Olds must bore
through dampness to fire,
                                        or that the morning
drags at my ankles and we've all worn
the same colour for days and puddles lie like
minefields and even skunks smell of water,
or that my left shoulder is three
months older than my right,
                                        or that bells
shiver where they chime or millions
of creatures a week old don't believe you ever were
or that the berries look wan and even spruce
pine for you,
                    or that the junkyard is a ferocious
green from the grass up, the crows
mistrust each other, the press
prints tracts of pain and you are neither here
nor there –
                    but I ask you, page one in the book
of stars and planets, you for whom Crayola
invented yellow, you the nearest hot
spot, to give it up for all of us
who huddle in caves of rain, eyes
dull with water.

After Rain, a Man

1

He's in the trees getting
colder every sound. If his heart was yours
it would flash and cover, part beat part
shiver. Put the heat on, he wants to be found
in your misery, your beautiful air. Every three
years or so this happens, this May-
cold rain.

2

Like cones he's surrounded by empty paths,
throughway to Jesus if Jesus was an empty path.
Bring him to your census, count the one of him
a hundred times. Be his next page, the size
of his contentment.

3

Be blue, a thought revealed, something he can
brighten in. But keep it simple,
fewer words longer through the line.

4

A year's enough to rethink
an afternoon. He'd rather feel you
than himself. He's warm but no
closer to you.

5

What else can I say
to love which like an alley
leads away.

WIND, FEBRUARY

My friends are together again, a dozen
in the doorway at once, scarves ragged, dresses
new. My company of coats and arms. None of us
arrive without a first word spoken, licked,
kissed to another, considered deeply, carried
to a house at the edge of a white field.

I didn't know the wind had red hair until I saw her.
I didn't know I'd live half-invisible, my blood
keeping time. I must tell my son and daughters
the ways I feel air today which could be any day
a window opens, wind makes sense in snow.

The wind bruises
our bodies with wild cards, ace
of spades first. Eight or nine of us take turns
losing. Lucky the wind's leaving town. We can win
among ourselves at the games we know.

We walk the same paths, my friends and I,
leading to each other.

February, Prayers for an Eastern View

I can see my Oldsmobile across the parking lot facing
east I can see my Oldsmobile.

"I am the true vine," writes Arvo Pärt about my Oldsmobile.

I can't believe the size of the music the size of the field I should be
fifty flakes into the woods by now looking to land, my Oldsmobile.

A woman across the hall opens her door, another way to speak the urge
to Oldsmobile.

In a thousand pages I haven't finished a single word. O Glory, I can't
build that word from the frame within my body, my syndromes, my art
until I sleep against my keyboard, waking up to find these words
about my Oldsmobile.

If I *look* I'm not, if I *see* I don't, my ego faces east, lit, simple.

How many chances do we get in this Oldsmobile?

What you can't do won't hurt, unless it locks you up inside. Climb in
through the back door, the window is expecting you. Stale face of old
loving, I'm with you, Oldsmobile, making out in the sparkin' lot.

A man should spend his life tracing the silhouette of every spruce, the
course of every flake of snow, the line of every sight. He should know
impossibility, certainty. He should shade his days by the slightest of
degrees, knowing his work was not and shall not be.

One morning in the drivetrain, a crescendo startles the buried seed,
chicka-dee-dee-dee, my Oldsmobile.

After awhile the cold. Sooner the wind. With effort give up the sentence of things, tremble in the breath-tracks, the to/from, the Oldsmobile.

A call, then an hour or two no answer answers, a swearing-against. Bells, a bell, bells-mobile.

Two hands at home feel the breath touch the lips the keys open lightly for the next word asking for it.

Dark shape, the white of things. Breath-mobile.

My Cockaigne

cockaigne: imaginary land, from Old French: land of delicacies;
from Middle Low German: small fancy sugar cake.
See kak-2 in Appendix.*

* GERMANIC ROOT: A ROUND OBJECT, DISK.

or just think "Big Rock Candy Mountain,"
the depression-era hobo's lament

The streets flash with a skin of new cars remembering
the first rain from a wounded sky. And grass
thickens old men at monuments. Everyone's office fills

with money and money floats by like lilacs rising from the pages
of a book, an answer of lilacs, look of lilacs multiplied.
Landlocked admirals name their mighty vessels

for misspelled words, *The Havuc, The Grilla, The Afeard.* Walls
of basements overflow, break out in posies, swell with golden
debris. A new building floods at its cross-section and heroes of eros

meet there, posing next to flowers, pressing closer, each naked
as the day the other was born. We agree on how
we're managing, *Department of Love*

on our left-front doors, me a memo you lick. Splinters of rain
stick me to you. Mud, thick, swirls on the cover of a lengthy
book, mandelas aplenty. On every table fruit glistens, no life is still.

The rain's a winner, easily picked. Schoolchildren pour
from the entranceways late for the goodness of their next step.
I take in breath through the eyes, no wonder they shine

in the park. Everyone's skin stays pure as moments
of birth when the womb empties, the mother cries and the father
has never felt the world so intensely. From the highest tower there *is*

a highest tower under which blood swerves its watery eyes, mock-
feudal eyes, wise to the water miles from here. Every this and that's
a jaunty tune for her majesty. Liquor's made of rivers that

pour round the bend.

Crow Town

A little place not too far away,
near as that smudge in the corner of your eye.
The light's so raw your eyes ache and at happy hour you eat
your chicken wings raw. That's how they do it
down in Crow Town.

In Crow Town you pull the top
off a sandwich, carry it to Thirteenth
Avenue, if you're lucky, squawking like
black Echos on the road that gets you
nowhere down in Crow Town.

In Crow Town when you're cold (and you're always
cold) you pull a shadow over yourself. Heaven
is someone else's egg in Crow Town, where afternoon's
an afterthought, and everyone's the captain of a ship
sunk belly-first in tar, for a good time call
1-800-BLACKNESS, that'll get you through.

Down there they give you the hard crow / soft
crow, lock your eyes, frisk you
for felonies, make sure you've got some.
You don't remember dreaming but wake up
eyeless, out of love, the by-laws of your heart
repealed. You have no rights unless you're wrong.

On the fierce bandstand of treeless nights the singer
scats with a knife in her back, the tenorman plays
a broken horn, the drummer taps, taps
nails into his own thin arms all night
wasting away and back, down in Crow Town.

In Crow Town the cathedral's a burn barrel, cossacks hang
ragged over unholy pools and beware the black hoods
on the filthy coins of Crow Town.

The only way to get there is carried in someone's mouth.
No boys, no girls, no pretty
tunes there, grandmas nothing but hags
in trees. Most of the time there's only *you*
in Crow Town.

IV

The next day nothing but heat again,
it's heat again,
the sky is.

Say, No More Silence

If you say the word *silent*,
you're not. If you think it, you're not. If you
paint it with your eyes closed, maybe. One leaf
in a breeze beside another – sure,
and lots more, silence closer than temperature.
Flies circle. See what
happens in hard light? The men are silent
as rooms, the women as underwater. This is
the silence that lives here.

More Silence

Water is surface a kingfisher breaks, a puff of what
water would be, were there any sound. All motorboats
shut off, their wakes quiet as beds. The insects
bump into reeds, I guess. There's no
telling.

I hear screaming out my window,
see mouths locked that way, bark
ripping the terror from trees, an empty road,
sunlight a gag on the forest, a frame
of breezes nothing blows.

The silence of rowing carries for miles.
Reflected trees seem forty feet deeper
than any sound. Even that cut-up of a moon
can't say *boo* to you. Mute, might as well be.
Blank lines I write to you, silent readings
I give to you, repeating myself.

Wind Essay

for twenty-five marks I say the wind
is a dried leaf splitting north by northwest over

the parking lot. One minute you're chilled,
the next hot, the one after that

all the plastic chairs have blown over except
the one you're on. No transition

takes you like the wind, just one
of many details. Prisoners, you are,

in the black bars of its room.
You can't see

anything but the truth dust brings.
Wind is both the next and previous

page, subject and verb, what chance
do words have in their ruled lines.

The wind is so obvious I skip
half my classes, still pass.

Advice to First-year English Students Ready to Read a Poem

You find yourself in a *book* and you're pulled
to the page ahead or the one behind.
You may not be able to shake free.
Keep on hitting what you can't see but keep on hitting.
Think of arriving at night, by yourself, not sure where
you'll sleep. Find yourself in words that don't
do what you want them to do (again,
do what you want them to do).
Embrace the person next to you, trying
to remember where you've been.
Sense the start-up of motors
in faraway alleys, press your hands
firmly over your eyes but a moment later
remove them. Open what you know.
(Behind you, someone has snapped her fingers.)
Refuse to be rescued by the bottom of the page.
The words *I don't like it* and *boring*
have just been used for the last time.
You're no singer but you harmonize
and your Golden Lab named Beaver will worry
but then lie down.

You will find the poem
lighter this way.

Anecdote of the Readers

I

By the time I get to my office door,
a dozen readers cluster there
copying the poem I'd posted. *Bad enough we have to*
read it, they say. *Now we have to*
write it down too. I sympathize but
cannot get through the clipboards and pens
to my desk where the next poem wants
to find itself found. *Can't you write anything*
shorter? one reader asks. *I liked that*
thing you wrote in September. And the readers
continue to copy. I hear their hands move
their eyes, my own words slip from their pens.
Come back later, the readers tell me.
We might have questions.

In ten minutes another thirty or so
readers have arrived, blocking
the hall outside my office. *What's that*
word after "airbrush," someone hollers
from back of the pack, which continues
to grow until I can see only
the top row of cindercrete over my door for all
the reading going on. *My God, what we do*
for grades, I hear a reader say. She's been elbowed
above the eyes. She bleeds but continues to read
with the other eye, half-words at a time.

2

Sunday afternoon before the Rider game
readers in sweatpants pass the door and pause,
bend over their backpacks, pull out a pen
to copy another poem. *Let's hope it's called*
"Countdown to Kick-off" a reader says.

They imagine a game, a western semi-final –
minus three Celsius, thirty-seven thousand fans.
The teams exchange big plays early.
Drives fail, receivers cannot hold on.
The players huddle around an injured lineman.
The readers huddle around the poem, concerned.
Some of them tap the poem gently, wish it
the best, and the game goes on, 7–3
Riders at the half.

As the Riders add to their lead in the second
half, readers leap and holler. The hallway
turns rowdy. Riders win 14–6 and readers trade
high fives, head butts, knuckle raps,
forearm shivers. On the plane home
Rider linemen hold four cans of beer
in one hand. Readers win
their poems.

3

The only time I can avoid readers
is to show up late at night, use my secret
password to enter the building. The hallway
is dark, silent. Approaching my office
I pause to savour the solitude of chairs,
a red-glowing exit light. Free
of readers at last! I step smartly
toward my door to collect the poems
forming inside.

At that moment a bullhorned voice from above
says *Step back from the door* and a brilliant shaft
of light bores into me through the skylight. A line
of commando readers descends from an N-407
Bell helicopter, their clipboards
gleaming. Soon I'm cuffed and led away
to the compound where readers recline
with their binders open. *What are you
saying in this poem,* their leader says, *and what
do you want with us?*

Afternoon After My Son's Grad

The parking lot quarter full of shadows,
flags on top of the Travelodge point
south and east, the clouds in pieces
ladled once or twice.

Tom at his mother's house disappears
downstairs all afternoon until the sun
stirs that land he calls
sleep and he rouses, climbs the stairs,
sits at the kitchen table with his Kodak 7430
to view the pics he'd taken the night before.

A night doesn't forget something like that –
fifteen kids up all night to breakfast
at Tom's place, numb to sky-high in an instant
and back, until they all go home to bed.

The landlord drives his lawn tractor
to the dumpster to empty his grass,
parks at the building door,
goes inside for coffee. Afternoon
reaches its quietest point, the grads
move on to summer, first
a couple of days' rest and this afternoon's
sharp hot sun.

Birds in the High Trees Refuse Bread One Sunny Day in July

crumbbird
breadlight

treecrumb
birdbread

lighttree
birdcrumb

lightbread
crumbtree

breadbird
treelight

(a true story)

Ten Missing Pieces

1
yes/no I know I can't but
want to see/kiss
you closer that
fooling you feel is mine up/down
your arm

2
walking where we walked
the other day I look for where you still
might be you 'n blue the sky over

3
boy again driving to Calgary after you
I damn near had to

4
every piece of paper says
I'm saving you up

5
you're on the map un-
folding in my hands

6
I don't believe our
lips have met today

7
lines get longer the longer you're gone
see how that one wants to?

8
now that I'm weary I
sleep for you

9
I'm
without you

10
I am the
secret you are

Praying For Rain

Dry has always meant
yellow grass a plague
of cusses on the land.

What do you have to do to get
rain around here my throat's
crumbling for lack of you
pouring it on a dry
kind of dry kind
of dry.

*

Pretend you're the business end of a quarter mile
of four-inch pipe fitted with rainbirds ready
to fly at my drylids, rave and burst from pumped
thunder like pauses from noise. I'm me, part meek,
surrendering to your might, your maybe.
What I'm missing is you.

*

Ozonized horseman, cross the boreal forest
from your natural source, your arty well.
Leave hoof-shaped pools, the feeling
we've been lucky again. Give me
an eruption. Finger me in showers,
lick me where the sun don't.

*

This wind gets me nowhere in fact there isn't
a wind my mistake it was a breath between crows
spooking cornstalks. I could hope less and feel you
more let you make your motions
moisten the garden of ash
that's left these days.

*

Take away this word said of wines said of
cocktails and eyes said of babies and dust taking
off after crows said of wit of the opposite
of wet said of beetles waiting
in the mouth of a tunnel grasshoppers
stalking a flaming wind this word
that leaves me.

*

I'll pencil the nimbus in this frightening
blue carry on meanwhile in pen
smoking again pencil-thin ash seeding
rain across these spaces twirled
erasures that pressure you
to fall.

*

You want to be a small quieter instrument coming
over us one of a hundred voices in a field three
miles from here to you a pip-
squeaking fiddle you so shy around shadows correct
yourself when the sun comes out nod like
petunias in sun or part sun humming.

*

I'm timing the chug of you
getting here sweat
listening treetops loaded
with caws. Be a record July
get high and loaded sprint
fifty metres then
fall like halves on other
halves finishing.

Stan Still's Book of Sadness

He has a dark look anyway at times.
— SINCLAIR ROSS, *As For Me and My House*

Chapter One

A grim suit rides with my shadows into town.
Some posse, sadness and the boys, five or six
abreast, somber hombres keeping
an eye on me, and they'd better.

Chapter Two

Every new shirt I wear
I'm more or less blue, wearing my sad
colours out one door, in another, my throat
and shoulders covered with it. I must admit
at times women love a sad man but that's no
reason to be a woman. *Get over it* she says. *Don't*
wear your sadness out on me.

Chapter Three

I first got sad in the '50s, no complaints about
boyhood but that's when I learned to be,
as they say on Children's Hour, left behind
when the Happy Train pulls away, call it
the tag end of what I'd heard was happy.
The memories are good but I hold them badly.
I think I'm in the wrong damn order.

Chapter Four

I whistle for a pet bird,
three of them fly straight over.
A particularly vibrant stem of grass
rips free and presents itself
before I know my mouth is dry.
Day-sayers perjure themselves saying *rain*
in their testimony. These are
former effects I just now
write down.

Chapter Five

We see by people's eyes the sadness
they carry. The entire face
aligns to eyes and posture.
Soon giant pines begin to lean
and out on the track all the runners race forever
only half-way around.
A blue trash barrel looks like silk, the air's so sad.

Chapter Six

Not to over-do it but I wear
a jacket of crows.

Chapter Eight

I say no, no, no, no too often.

V

I'll watch night's warning leading up to you,
it's up to you,
the sky is.

Hiding Places

In the minutes of committees that meet at 9:00 p.m.

the mind of a garden bent under a man

the point where one room becomes another

my dead father's oxfords

the moment of our last goodbye

twenty rungs down an imagined well

decisions about when to plow

the deep oil of a dark blue Dodge

a monk's imagination

an insomniac reflected

some other season

a quarter note sung tomorrow

pile of salvage from a burnt shed

the cast of a monarch's shadow on a shoe

I find you.

Listing to You

I want the passing fancy of words
that rhyme with your name, the sweet
paths you follow, the mournful
dressing of your train.

I want the sentences you haven't
begun, that point where language
wipes its feet at the door.

I want that blanket-and-hat
wrap you see the stars in,
greeting them with your eyes,
your memory, I want
this and that I want to go on.

I offer to write whatever I can.
I offer tender loafing, that bread
I saw you with at breakfast.

I have reached my limit
of lines I begin.

Please copy this list down.
pin it to your secret wall.

Before Dark

I

The day's in hand, finishing a silent
tea, running once again out
of light beyond the angle of a roof.

Got the day shovelled off,
leaned all afternoon,
got clear.

2

One of the plain words, night always
knows what it means.

Night accumulates in prayers,
rows of switched-on lamps, rooms
and black books opened, in drinks
Larry pours. Night's no joke
but laughter's in it, someone goes
out to night and returns.

Every day reverses itself, a round
of headlights bouncing in the pines.

3

I see it coming but walk into it anyway, the night
in my eyes, memorized. I can taste my own belief
in snow. A sharp holler, no one's ever there.

Night is a mute sensation, I've heard.
Solo piano like a footstep strikes
and disappears. But someone else was here
with her hand to her face before the wind.

Few signs, a row of spruce trees.
Nothing's where it is.
How lovely the snow's face.

4

When you want to keep playing there's always light
though the puck grows tighter in its darkness
and against the tape on a stick cannot be seen
but felt and you continue to play,
snowbanks the whitest things,
sky the colour of a Leaf jersey with black on it.
With long passes hopeless you skate close together.
The rushes are bolder, this may be the last one
but the puck comes loose, play breaks the other way.
Everyone hollers for the last shot
and here it is, no, nowhere near the goal
which after all cannot be seen.
No goals let's just keep playing
and there's another rush.
You all skate in the same general direction
which is not home,
your stick ready in case the night itself
finds its way to you.

5

The moment from before to after dark
goes on and on every day, if day's the right
word for this time I keep an eye on, this moment
or whatever it is when the sky disappears
and all a roofline does is separate one
darkness from another.

Night's got day in its pocket.
Soon I'll be the only thing lit around here,
hanging on for dear light, welcoming
the last of it, my window open to afterlight,
the endless crossing over.

The Difference Between Night and Day

Not so many tractors at night. In their oily
sheds they cool, drip a little, breathe, free
of hands at last.

Night has strangers in it. I can't see their eyes.
When they speak it's only their mouths
I see, the bite of a few black words.

There's no such thing as moonburn.

Only my days, not my nights, are numbered. I'll live
forever at night, after bells, when I show you
my heart, and my heart refuels.

Nothing is open except whatever tells
one star from another.
And the whiteness on a gravel road.
And whatever's between us.
And the gash from which lightning bleeds.

There's no risk of day at night.
We kissed and all that.
We were new at night.

A Moth Story

Ronnie's first haircut
was not going well.
First he swallowed a moth
thinking it was a sunflower seed.

Then he lit a moth and smoked it
thinking it was half a joint.

Now he swallowed a lock of his own hair
thinking it was a moth.

I remember last night
a woman walked out of the prairie
sat down beside me at the fire
looking for what I call, but she wouldn't, *love.*

I said *breath* she said *body.*
I said *holy* she said *this hour*
and the next one or two
are the only times I don't feel alone.
I said *Are you a moth?*
Yes she said loosening what I see now as wings.
Walk lightly as you follow me inside.

All the way into the bedroom, I followed her.
We took turns capturing.
She liked me swatting whatever
my hungry arms could reach
with the Canada Day edition of the *Globe & Mail.*
Neighbours over the field could hear
the whumps of our persistence
and her husky flutter *Now go,*
get the flyswatter.

I got to know my own body last night.
She seemed to go up and down on me at the same time
in twenty-four places at once. I swear she meant
mid-air where she wanted me spinning
like I'd had too much to see. I kissed every
direction a wing could fly or a hand open.
I threw myself against two walls then
the same two again glimpsing wildly
the stars and wanting to say *o how beautiful*
crying only *o* as someone's arm smashed
the light to pieces

and in the darkness *o*
clear and gentle darkness
she lies still my lips
tasting grey.

Youngest Daughter, First Date

I stand before you tonight with no emotion
to speak of my daughter, age sixteen,
waiting downstairs for her young man.

Nothing dramatic in the movie I watch,
the dishes drying on the rack.
No vision whatsoever of her face
telling me yesterday a young man
would arrive tonight to take her away.
Purely neutral my reading of her panic
when her mom brings over the wrong makeup bag.
No need for the midday call to my own mother,
who says that's the way it was
with her three daughters.

No introspection
other than this poem.
These wounds on my hands – accidental.
Deep lesions – already there.
No exceptional urge to moan
in the basement near the furnace
and the rough concrete walls on which fathers
gouge the tally of hours, waiting
their daughters' return.

Four Songs Heard Across the Alley from a Parking Lot

1

A Topaz in a hurry trails
fragments, yellow paint.
Six men in matching
motorcycles, numerous screams,
broken tint of windows, cops,
delivery vans, cars needing work – all sounds
against the backs of stores.

Still the lot endures, leaks,
bloodies with oil and antifreeze,
hears a voice say "Well, I guess
I'd better put the broken glass away
if Dave's son is coming over," hears wind
ripping at crows.

This parking lot loves its colour, a tarred rose
smeared with mud left to harden.

2

In sun an alley softens, even dumpsters
look like a cousin you needn't
worry about, a function key you press
only to throw something away
and a lasting image of love that didn't last
while up on the balconies chairs break and pages
fly free, extreme wind the only time
you can't hear birds or feel them
shifting on your roof.

3

A block or so away in three
directions, more parking lots,
more scrap metal and landlords,
team buses, RVs not to mention
the bodies inside.

If not the parking lot the sky
in faraway colours, blacktop and blue,
clouds big as strip malls, ideas,
the sentiment of a man drinking tea.
Once in a while the sun films over
ultravioletly if that's
the right word, then crawls free,
forcing our shirts off again.

4

A way to get through is a beautiful thing.
As is this alley and a love that's true,
as is this alley where a driver yields
to a woman with garbage and
someone bangs a tennis ball,
tenants sip black tea.

5:30, skateboarders wear out
the concrete driveway sloping
to the loading dock, carry on past the hotel,
disappear into memory.

Night becomes the hero,
a blue so casual
its edges blacken, daughters and sons
running out of light, cooling,
and just like that a new moon
shivers into view.

Her Leaving

1

The broken man is left doubly naked, whiter
than he's ever been, no one sure what next
to touch – his eyes maybe his few
good bones or the surface he keeps
for a woman just here, just leaving. She took
part of his whiteness away, barely noticed
his mind on the spool of her unwinding.

The day leaves light behind, a moon
hooking left, slash of light
in water reflecting loudly in moons
broken, rough.

2

By morning all darkness in the man's body
drains to his lower right leg, digs in,
swells within the cast's hard frame.

No other place for darkness to go than where
it came from all night. He slept,
shadows rising up his thigh with a shiver
across his crotch through his chest hairs and out
the tops of his body.

The old lake was pretty quiet last night he says.
Now that you've gone, he thinks, but doesn't say.

VI

I guess by morning I'll know what's true,
the sky is true,
the sky is.

Windowing

Stan follows life, which follows Stan. Behind him
silence, in front of him air. Tap, tap, not air
but that pain he's pretty sure he imagines.

Here between the street and his heart
Stan has kept himself in the present
since yesterday. In the present Stan laughs
at the sight of the landlord losing
half a box of papers to the wind.

Here between the street and his heart
Stan has a moment of a crow's
moment of Stan, both of them victims
of sunset right now mustering
its last blue.

Closer, the petals of a lily
stutter a little. Closer yet,
love and other agonies
have left. His body is light
leaving a room.

Here between the street and his heart
he wants to get rid of himself
in the ribs of that blackening air.

One Morning in the Food Court Waiting for the Post Office to Open Observing the Old Men Gathered for Coffee, Wondering How I Can See You, Kissing You Smack on the Memory

The night the pauses drained from space
between us I should have known right then the *ex*
would fall on me, the shape of your bones first
attracting then accusing me (let's
be blunt) of kindness, generosity and other
terms, accusing me of passion old men feel
for lovers decades ago. Every time they look away
they see you, someone as close as you, a woman still
warm in their hands at night, as real as where
you came from, made up. The old men laugh, it takes
so long even now to see clear of you, a view
skinning a grey-white sky.

New Shoes

This morning I drove slowly
to work through half-
scraped windows wondering
how much or little to say
in my new shoes.

The shoe expands to fit the foot. I walked
Mom to the store along the duck-and-blackbird
path every half-day or so thinking
of you and faithful mothers.
Sixty years ago she worked
in the telephone office in Palmer. When Dad
phoned to say he'd be home everyone else
up the line heard the news. (Mom also
remembered Spike, her sister's
husband, a fighter pilot, who died
before the flowers he sent reached
his bride.) How can I
be happy. You were
that close.

Stan Still Considers His Absent Lover's Book

The table on which he's placed her book
opens one of its wings. The bottle of water
resting there bears at its surface
a hopeful tremor. A folded scrap of paper saying
the prairie begins to straighten
its crease a little. The pair of glasses, facing in,
as if taking a look from outside,
reveals a portion of the table
enlarged – how prairielike its contours! –
and half-arcs of water where the bottle was.
Three books occupy the opposite corner of the table:
Poetry for Men and Women, How to Think and Eat
Like a Poet, and *How to Wear a Poet's Shoes.*
Stan Still, who sits at the table,
has been wiping down the windowsills
in his boxer shorts and doing calisthenics –

all this because of her book,
the creatures embossed in its cover
which lifts from the table into his hands.

Stan Still's New Library

The first book, *Poetry for Men and Women,* gives
the usual enticements –
    keep your lid on but take it off after a while
    throw your language out there
    make yourself available.
Stan's fingers turn green by the time
he highlights it all.

The second book, *How to Think and Eat*
Like a Poet, proposes
a writer's typical day: go out, see how far you walk
today compared to yesterday, rinse a teapot,
attend to personal grooming. Time for a nap
and it's noon and you've done little
but written much.

The third book, *How to Wear a Poet's Shoes,*
really just a title so far, explains how
poets get around, what they look like and say
when they move. (Readers of this book
can contact poetshoes@gmail.com to find out more.)

Stan won these books at a poetry reading.
He thought he was getting *out* of the rain.
Stan doesn't know what to do with these books,
but they know what to do
with him.

Stan Still's Theory About Poets

Because longer poems pay
an extra thirty-five bucks, poets scribble like moths.
The poems creep to the next half-page,
line after line until the poems
fill the sky with shadow, the page
with birds, words, fragments of clouds, the marks
of poets in their fine hard books.

Instead of thirty lines, three hundred.
Instead of facts, myths. A man drinks
tea for a thousand years. A lily burns, water
restores its bloom. They'll write poems
for daylight, the poets, follow it to night. Give them lightning
they'll give it back letter-sharp, all elbows, running
roughshod over vertical. Give them thunder,
they're under it, counting how
long it rolls and when
unlike poets it comes to an end.

Or poets will grab onto the day, pull
just enough to slow it down, thus the lag
in poets' work between what happened
and when they write it.

They claim they're built for interruptions.
"It's part of what I do," they cry,
saluting a phone call, the eighth and ninth
innings of a ballgame on the radio, the need
for more beer. "If no one interrupts me,"
they say, "I can't get back to work."

And that's enough of that sort of thing for Stan.

Stan Sends Her an Outline of His Hand

here
put it on you
it just now shivered with my own small cries
hold it where you like a hand and move yourself to it
don't wait

hold it up
the hand is a big field
you remember from a year ago
they plowed over the old path
we'll have to start again
this ruled hand yours now
don't wait

at work make copies and spill them over yourself
on that two-handed loveseat in your office
then take me to the coffee shop for tea

take me
by this hand
don't wait

A True and Accurate Account in Plain Speech of Stan Writing to His Favourite Band

Every word Stan allowed into
his poor poem was being sung
at that moment by Alison Krauss.

Every idea he thought of,
the Krauss band, Union Station,
had already laid it down.

For the fun of it, Stan thought *Oldsmobile*
and other secret images but in every case
Krauss and her band played it.

Jerry Douglas on dobro.
Ron Block, Dan Tymchuk on guitars and banjo.
Krauss herself on violin.

Stan could see a good evening shaping up.
A simple evening,
light snow twenty below.

If Stan lost his place in his own thoughts,
wait a chorus or two and he's back in,
feeding, Stan thought, all harmony.

No matter how much Stan flattened out,
the songs continued to build,
maybe a tad pretty at times.

And just when he thought the instrumentalists
carried the band, Krauss would sing –
fiddling on his moments with her hands.

Stan doesn't care what he's doing as long as
he's doing this. All that would distract him
is the sun going down, or a knock on his door.

Alison Krauss and the band step away all this time,
come back with *loving you for good reason could be the wrong one*
and Stan begins to swing.

Songs For a Disappearing Moon

1

Old moonlight settles. Fresh snow leaves us
our pale songs. The old moon lifts
a degree or two from the grey-
orange tarnish, its vision blurred.

2

At the walls of the dreamed city, people gather
with tea, fruit, fragments of white cloth they twist
into landscapes, believing one day
a clearing will come, first a choir
of flawless trumpets, then a dignified
daylight sweeping its train along the aisles.

3

Sunrise opens south over yardlights
and a line of trees now distinct.
Moments later the old moon pales in its arc
to extinction south by southeast, a giving up
moon. The 7:40 from Canora sounds
the two-toned chord of an old moon, both on
and out of time, both dying, pitching
yoo-hoos one last time.

A Shape of Wind

For his drive north out of Southey, the wind blows a white hard field.
After that, more of it – blizzard of sun, wind tight as combs.

Someone told him to go ahead, expose inner and outer lives to each other,
but he'd never tried it, unless this was it. Only gravestones are at home
in this wind; Stan feels like dying, returning to the lost town.

Pages sixty to seventy-two of Stan's notebook are filled with such expressions
of earth, notes in a driven hand. I doubt if they'll stay in this order,
Stan reckons. They're road signs, pointing somewhere else.

Oops, he remembers his lover's laugh, looks in the mirror, is laughing.

A jet shoots through, near as Stan's right shoulder. That's Canada-US
weaponry for you. We sprawl like an old white dog in their pickup truck;
they run their stinking fingers through our air. Give me a sky full of
air force trainers out of Dafoe circa 1944. Give me *our* boys.

Watching the fields, think brown and white. Or black and white in colour.
Think stubble-snow, trees so bare. Think Mounties (a.k.a. wind)
springing from Fedderson Road.

The highway heaves its hours, thermometer holding at minus twenty-one,
sun at high, light at a constant howl. Stan rededicates himself to this country
of wind, and a school bus, and the odd crow straining, all of this already old.

Stan Opens a Letter Meant for Someone Else

Congratulations! You have won
this summer moment. You have won a new heart
and a shadow twice as long. You have won a fire,
an iron ring to hold it and smoke that blows clear.

No more reading every line
as if she was in it, every voice
as not quite hers. You will not be caught
looking away, you will not be lost.

Yes, you have won a clear view
after love. Not sure? Yes you are!
You have won yourself back.

And look, you have won a new moon!
See how it knows you. No more lover in the field
or in your mind, no more projections
of your lover in the breeze.

The moon has carried her away.

Acknowledgements

A tip of the cap to Laura Burkhart, Jill Morgan and Francie Greenslade, who shivered through the drafts of many of these poems. Brenda Schmidt helped me talk my way to Stan Still. Elizabeth Philips gave an earlier version of the manuscript a darned good reading. I'm grateful to the Saskatchewan Arts Board, Saskatchewan Writers/Artists Colonies and Luther College at the University of Regina for various forms of support that helped me produce this work. Thanks to Greg Maillet for Dante.

Earlier versions of some of these poems have been published in *Arc, event, Grain, The Malahat Review, The Fiddlehead, From the Ear of the Heart: Writing from St. Peter's Abbey,* and *Prairie Fire,* and broadcast by CBC Saskatchewan. Thanks to the editors and producers. A few poems first appeared in my own workplace series, *Poems for an Office Door,* published outside Room 218, Luther College.

"A Moth Story" won second place in the 2006 Saskatchewan Writers Guild Short Manuscript competition.

Feel free to contact poetshoes@gmail.com with your comments.

Finally, I thank my razor-sharp editor, the wonderful Jeanette Lynes, for bringing me closer to my own work.

ABOUT THE AUTHOR

Gerald Hill has released three previous poetry collections: *The Man From Saskatchewan,* published by Coteau Books; *Heartwood;* and *Getting To Know You,* which won the Saskatchewan Poetry Award in 2004. Published widely in literary journals and anthologies, he has also written the text for a collection of biographies and photographs called *Their Names Live On: Remembering Saskatchewan's Fallen in World War II,* 2001.

Born in Herbert, Saskatchewan, Gerald Hill has moved to Regina three times, most recently in 1995, amid stops in Calgary, Rocky Mountain House, Papua New Guinea and Edmonton. He completed an undergraduate degree in Education from the University of Calgary, a diploma in Creative Writing at David Thompson University Centre, Nelson, British Columbia, and a graduate degree in English at the University of Alberta. He now teaches English at Luther College at the University of Regina. You can reach him at his web site and blog, *www.geraldhill.ca* and *poetshoes.blogspot.com.*